TIPS FOR TEACHERS

TIPS FOR TEACHERS

❧❀❧

WHAT YOU DIDN'T LEARN IN COLLEGE ABOUT THE CLASSROOM

Kindest regards...
Teaching is the Key.

by Mary J. Howell

Mary J. Howell
2/08

edited by
Howell Enterprise

ISBN: 978-0-9800942-0-6

Manufactured in the United States of America

This book is intended for educational purposes.

Dedication

With tenacity and perseverance Maggie Taylor touched so many lives with her spiritual strength and zest for life and helping others. Living for 100 years and four months, my grandmother instilled in me the importance of believing in yourself and trusting in a higher being.

To my grandmother-Maggie Taylor, Mother-Naomi Bush, and all of my family members and special friends who have had to participate and endure all of my creative ventures. Thank you.

A special thanks to my husband, Taft for all the patience, love, and support given during the time spent before publication.

Contents

ESSENTIAL CLASSROOM TACK

✑✿✑ **28** ✑✿✑

To Grade or Not to Grade?
Record Keeping
Documentation (Anecdotal Record Keeping)
Break Times, Recess and Hall Passing
Substitute Teacher Planning

PARENTAL INVOLVEMENT

✑✿✑ **37** ✑✿✑

Working With Parents
Newsletters

TEACHER PROFESSIONALISM

✑✿✑ **40** ✑✿✑

Benefits to Teacher Organizations
Goals and Professional Development
Stress and Teaching

CHECKLIST 44
Successful Activities, Task and Procedures

Preface
by
Joann Gilford
Retired Tulsa Public Schools
Teacher, Supervisor, Principal, Reading Specialist,
and Consultant

Never before has it been more urgent that we understand the basic needs which motivate children's behavior so that our style and strategies adequately address the diversity that is today's norm. This book is designed to assist teachers in the beginning of their career to lessen the possibilities of frustration, uncertainty and confusion upon their first teaching assignment.

Having been a new teacher—had I been given this material, I am certain I would have felt more secure and better informed as a teacher/manager in the classroom. One of my life long observations of teacher preparation has been the lack of feedback that provides one with solid information that automatically works. How we begin is usually how we end if not closely monitored and the recipient of weekly assessments in instruction, leadership and camaraderie. Often we are communicated the essentials to help one feel knowledgeable in the district goals and objectives without relevant examples that work.

This books purpose provides ideas, and working principles which clearly define how we go from point A to B. It incorporates tips that will strengthen professional ethics and build stronger character. The books language is simple and tips are easy to remember and apply. The aim of the author seeks to enhance your understanding of what the teaching profession is all about.

I am impressed with the teaching activities checklist and think you will be too. Simplicity is always of value when so much is required. I encourage you to add this book to your daily routine.

INTRODUCTION

The greatest satisfaction in the world is to attend college, receive your teaching degree, go in for a job interview and hear the fantastic words "You are hired!"

After getting your teaching job and being assigned a classroom, you walk into a barren classroom in August and will be expected to transform that room into an attractive, welcoming, educational environment.

The challenge of creating an educational niche for students will be your haven for students and your private domain for educational enrichment. The challenge of getting your room ready for students can be exciting if you know the direction in which your are heading. Knowing the components of setting up a room can be mind boggling. Are you ready for the challenge? Your philosophy, expectations, organizational skills and creativity will immediately be on display to students, parents, teachers, and your new principal.

Teaching is the profession that touches and prepares individuals to pursue their career choices. Welcome to the challenge of educating students for the world of tomorrow!

Mary J. Howell

Passion for Teaching

A passion for teaching means you are forever focused on how you can improve your skills to set up a conducive room environment that will allow all the students to grow academically, mentally, socially, and emotionally. As a teacher, you adapt arms similar to an octopus with the tentacles serving as the many arms and hats you will wear during your teaching career. Not only will you be a teacher, but you become counselor, surrogate mom, role model, fashion setter, confidant-within legal limits, nurse, observer, and interpreter.

The passion for teaching will diminish the drive for money. The educational arena may not be the most lucrative field to enter into, but it is the most rewarding field—for it assist mankind in its endeavor. As you teach students they will be like diamonds in the rough and you will get the opportunity to teach and polish them into rare stones. One of the key variables to remember is that all students are capable of learning-but not all students will learn the same things at the same time and on the same day. Your patience, drive, and determination to help students excel, will be your final reward. To see the joy and experience an exciting feeling of accomplishment. When the light bulb goes on in a students head—you have accomplished your goal of student's mastery. That is an exciting feeling.

Use the contents of this book to guide, to inspire, clarify, and challenge you to teach individual students according to their needs and abilities. This book is not just designed for first year teachers; it can be used for educational classes and seminars, also a helpful guide for student teachers. The experienced teacher can use this as a reinforcer of instructional and classroom skills update.

SCHOOL SETTING
(ADMINISTRATOR AND STAFF)

Relationships with Teachers

When you embark on the educational scene, don't be afraid to ask questions or ask a fellow teacher for suggestions or help. New teachers are provided a mentor teacher to help them to make the transition easily. The mentor teacher is there to help advise, provide suggestions, and guide you through the teaching process. If you are a new teacher just entering the profession, you will participate in a teacher mentoring program. Utilize the services of the mentor teacher. If you are a veteran teacher in a new environment, establish a relationship with a buddy teacher. Although you may have worked for the school district and transferred to a new site, administrators will establish different procedures for their school—you will need to know the policies and procedures for that site.

Many new teachers go into the classroom and experience difficulty in the theories in the book and cannot adjust to the real classroom. The book and the actual learning environment did not match. This discourages teachers, some become distraught and quit. Dare to be different, ask questions. Be curious and be observant. You can learn so much from teachers around you. Notice how teachers handle discipline and interact with their students. Notice the teacher to teacher interactions and pay close attention to how the other classrooms look in the building. Once you have been assigned a building, you will immediately find out who are considered master teachers. Don't hesitate to emulate master teachers. Remember you are in the classroom to teach, you are not there to be a student's best friend.

Veteran teacher's had to develop their skills. Don't be intimated by veteran teachers—learn to seek their advice. You too will have an opportunity to develop, grow, and gain confidence in your classroom delivery. Teacher success will be measured by how successful students progress in the classroom. Each student will be unique and it will be your responsibility to discover the talents and help them to excel. Remember you are in the classroom to teach and not to be a buddy to the students. Teach and provide them with the skills to succeed.

Principal Interaction

Your first interaction with the principal is important. Learn to make polite conversation and develop rapport immediately. You should realize that your future educational aspirations are in the hands of your new administrator. He/she will be evaluating your classroom performance. The principal is your superior, evaluator, and final decision maker if you will have continued employment with the school district.

There are several reasons for principal's to visit your classroom. At the beginning of the school year, principal's check on class sizes, observe students behavior, and many stop just to show support. Don't become tense when the principal comes to your room unannounced. Students were on task, you had just finished an absolutely wonderful lesson—the principal enters in the door. The students were not engrossed in academics. Principals are smart enough to know what is going on in the classrooms. Many new teachers are uncomfortable with their first principal. Often the fear is unwarranted.

As soon as you have prepared you room attractively and conducive for learning, invite the principal to visit your room. This will help you to ease the jitters of the principal coming into the room for evaluation. Early visits by the principal will help to calm your nerves and help prevent the paranoia of the principal showing up and the students' behavior not being up to par.

Once the principal has evaluated you and you have your conference, ask the principal if there are suggestions for improvement. Request to visit other classrooms in the building and if necessary, ask permission to go to another site. This request does not admit failure—you are wanting to get assistance for greater growth and teacher preparation. When you are not sure, continue to use the master teacher to strengthen your teaching skills.

Always organize your classroom and instructional delivery to best meet the needs of the students within your classroom. Use quality instructional times and optimum time frames to get the most work from the students. Proper use of textbooks to assist, extend and provide knowledge to students in an optimum learning environment is crucial. Once the organization and management skills are mastered, the principal's presence in the room will be welcomed. Discipline and organizational skills precedes learning. Gain your instructional confidence so that you will demonstrate to the principal, parents, colleagues, and visitors that you are an excellent teacher.

Residency Teacher Program

Depending upon the state in which you teach, there are different terms to identify first year teachers and programs that assist with success the first year. First year teachers are provided with mentor teachers. The mentor teacher's responsibility is to assist you in areas in which you need growth, explanations and planning. Don't be afraid to ask your mentor teacher for assistance. There should be time provided in which you and the mentor teacher will discuss your classroom techniques and approaches to meeting your students' needs. Sometimes out of fear, first year teachers are afraid to ask questions.

Key School Personnel

Though the principal is the site administrator in the building, there are other key personnel you need to develop a positive relationship with for success. The **school secretary** is the one you need to establish rapport. The secretary will provide you with supplies, textbooks, and important building information. In some schools' you will need to go through the school secretary to get an appointment to see the principal. Ask the secretary about school supplies, textbooks and faculty meeting dates. Some secretaries are from the community in which you are working, they can provide you with valuable information about students and parents. Weigh all facts—sometimes information you receive will not be applicable to your interaction with parents.

The **custodian**—establish a working rapport with the custodian immediately; he/she is an important team player. This is the person who will clean your room and provide year long maintenance to your classroom. When you need furniture or other items, the custodian will assist you with the needs. At the beginning of the teaching day, spend a few moments making sure your room is in order. Repeat this task at the end of the day. The custodian will appreciate the extra effort you have taken in making his/her job easier. When you first start teaching, spend a few moments making sure your room is fairly decent at the end of the day. The custodian will love you for the extra effort you put into keeping the room clean.

The **school counselor**—will have many roles in a building. Develop a relationship with the counselor. If they have been at that site for a period of time, they can be a tremendous help-if you experience difficulties or concerns with students. The counselor can share with you if students have personal issue that would interfere with their school successes. When approaching the counselor for assistance or emotional issues— remember don't forget that parents are sending their most prized possession to school and may need your help and advice.

Room Organization & Classroom Management

Once you open the door and walk inside the room, it becomes your classroom. Your mind immediately focuses on:

- Where to place your desk
- Room atmosphere you want to create
- What will I put on the boards or how the room will become attractive for learning

That includes classroom arrangement, bulletin boards, chairs, tables, interest centers and books. These factors will depend on the grade level of students and how many subjects you will be responsible for teaching in that classroom. The room should be conducive for students to be actively engaged in learning. Be aware of the importance of bulletin boards and other room enhancements.

Bulletin Boards

Boards in the classroom can serve as instructional tools, interactive displays, student activity centers, or task boards. Board ideas can be quite challenging for new teachers. There are ready made commercial materials for every school event or activity. There are a variety of books which assist you in making attractive bulletin boards or other enhancements for the classroom. In preparing for the beginning of the year, decide how you will utilize the boards. Designate which boards will be specific learning concepts at the very beginning and develop ideas or concepts to illustrate the concepts. A good method for designing your boards is to draw an outline of the boards and decide on paper what concepts/ideas you will put up for display. Grade level will help you decide key usage of boards, such as: monthly calendars, upcoming events, seasonal art work, student display skills, concepts, and task boards. Use the bulletin boards as a visual springboard for creative writing and problem solving activities.

Commercial Art Displays

Pre-designed packages in which material is placed for easy use and assembly, can be purchased at any school supply or discount store. It is just a matter of knowing what you would like to use for bulletin board displays. Some attractive or personalized boards are made by educators using an opaque machine or a machine that enlarges or copies a variety pictures for you to design. Many of the new printers and computers can be used to do excellent board displays. If you have a teacher's resource room, there may be an Ellison machine available. The Ellison machine will allow you to cut out die patterns and lettering to put on your boards.

Task Boards

A design or character is used in a spot in the classroom that identifies a skill that students are expected to achieve. Gradually during the weeks to come, the same symbol is utilized up with a different skill or procedure for students to follow. This is an excellent way to assist students to become independent learners, follow instructions and provides for acceleration and individual advancement in the classroom.

Storage Files and Educational Materials

As the months pass, you will accumulate materials that will assist you in the classroom with upcoming units, events, or teaching strategies. You will need to decide early in the process how you will file, store, and retrieve materials. Your plans for storage should include:

> • A file drawer, preferably near your desk, would allow you to store materials until it can be sorted and placed in an organized manner. Make sure you have storage for—magazine ideas, hand-outs from colleagues, mail fliers, and newspaper clippings.

- Storage area—may be a room, closet, or large cabinet, or you may have to use boxes and dividers for units and monthly events. If space allows, you may have boxes for every month—all materials, handouts, fliers, magazine articles should be stored annually.

Tip

How the boards will be used is the most important question that you will need to decide. When someone enters your classroom make sure you display what you want them to feel.

- Bulletin Board essentials-magic markers, crayons, glue sticks, scissors, pencils, chalk, paint, seasonal wrapping paper, wallpaper, fabric, and just about anything that you are willing to use to create a message on the board. Your creativity can abound when designing bulletin boards.
- Letter machines or pre-cut letters and symbols—time saving machines are available in some schools in which you can use dies to cut letters and various symbols. This is a time saver in which the letters can be cut quickly, neatly, and uniform. Some machines have dies for each month.

Check with your building representative to find out if the district has a professional development center. Some school districts have a Professional Development Center where teachers can work and make attractive school display.

Consider the method you use to store materials—all ways store immediately. It is so easy to misplace or forget to put all the pieces to a display together.

Learning Centers

Centers are designated areas in the classroom that complement identified skills for student mastery. Materials placed in the center can be art ideas, vocabulary building concepts, creative writing activities, brain teasers, math puzzles, dictionary or library skills development, historical or language oriented skills, historical facts, and self-analysis concepts. The list is endless. Some centers can be task oriented for the purpose of teaching the most difficult to the easiest concepts. Centers should be pre-planned and adaptable to the specific grade levels.

Non-Teaching Chores

College preparatory courses do not prepare you for the many non—teaching chores that are required of teachers. Many of the activities are pre-requisites before class can start. In order to avoid frustration for you and to get office request completed, you should be aware of some requested tasks: collecting money list, student telephone numbers and addresses, locker list, bus riders, classroom schedules, hall supervision times, playground duty schedules, cafeteria duty times, Xeroxing papers for classes, designing hall bulletin boards, decorating classroom doors, in—school meetings, serving on groups for improvement plans, and school district meetings.

Be prepared—suggestions for organization: keep copies of student roster list—use when you have to send student information to the office or turn in checklist.

ℸ IP
It is always best to keep copies of repetitive task. It will make is easier to retrieve and less frustrating to keep doing the same form repeatedly. Keep a master calendar readily available; and copies of schedules handy. The reality is that sometimes materials that you are requested to turn into the office area is lost. Always keep a copy of materials that you send to the office to avoid conflict.

What to Do When Problems Occur?

When the students arrive in your classroom, you will have a diverse group whose needs must be met physically, mentally, and socially. Learn the names of the students' immediately. You can gain control quickly when you can call a students' name for both positive and negative activities and situations.

There will be a variety of social needs that need to be addressed. If you revert back to the Child Psychology and Developmental classes you attended in college; you will note that some student will exhibit all the symptoms of Maslow's hierarchy of needs. Depending on the school in which you work, some sites will have free breakfast programs—the school is addressing a physical need.

Often teachers panic and blow an uncomfortable student situation out of proportion. If experiencing classroom difficulty, isolate the area of concern. Step back and be objective in what you think the real issue is. In analyzing discipline problems, separate the act from the student. The way we feel toward students, prevent us from looking at a situation objectively. Problems and situations cannot be dealt with when you are angry. Should you loose control, calm down, and do not be confrontational. A hasty decision can haunt and cause trouble forever—if not carefully handled.

Once the problem has been identified, seek solutions:

- Look at the complete picture—check to see if someone else is involved.
- Don't be afraid to consult with other teachers or the counselors expertise regarding the student. Utilize the counselor as a part of the staff; they can work with you to resolve student situations.
- If you think you need your principal's advice or involvement, do not hesitate to visit. Should the

principal not be in agreement with your actions it may require seeking the aid of the Teachers Union. Consult your building teacher representative for further information.

There are different needs and characteristics related to elementary, middle and high school students. Their physical, intellectual, psychological and social needs will differ. Students will gradually move from self centered behavior and attitudes to social and peer pressure behavior as they go from elementary to the high school setting.

Keep current with new approaches and theories and be willing to adjust and re-vamp classroom procedures to meet the needs of the students who are currently in your classroom. Many districts will offer professional development workshops on classroom management or approaches to discipline. Make and attend workshops that are beneficial to your growth. You will always gain insight and new methods to change instructional techniques that may or may not be working to your satisfaction. Get a new perspective on issues that bother you.

Essential Classroom Task

Curriculum and Teacher Editions, Distinct Goals, Missions and State mandated materials—check with your department chair or leader, or curriculum person for your site to find out if there is a prescribed curriculum or materials that should be used in the classroom. Some sites have prescribed materials that need to be posted in the classroom as well as books the teacher's should be using. Find out about these things early—before you start doing lesson plans.

To Grade or Not to Grade

Grading papers can be your worst nightmare if you do not set up a system for grading the students' class work. Your grading patterns should be established for the students at the beginning of the school year. There should be a clear cut, well identified grading scale. Recommended procedures are:

- Explain the grading pattern to the students and post the grading scale in the room. Before classes start, ask your grade level team, department chairman, or principal what method of grading is utilized in the building.

28

- In the high schools, a clear cut manner of grading should be incorporated. As assignments vary from the clear cut true and false format to essay, where points equal certain grades—inform the students in advance. As students become older; they will question on why a grade was given. Students sometimes will challenge the method in which you grade—be ready to address.

- As you mark student's papers, show respect for the students. Putting poor grades in large letters in red can destroy a student's self-esteem. Blatant F-for failure or U for unsatisfactory work in the upper right hand corner two inches high in red pen-this form of shock grading should be discouraged. A message is being sent that the work is unsatisfactory as well as letting the whole class see the unsatisfactory grade. Students anticipate the return of testing papers, there is an automatic exasperation of defeat, embarrassment, and a decline in self esteem. This is an unfair method of grading.

Grading with comments-a very acceptable method in which students can be motivated by the comments placed on the paper. This is a personal communication between the teacher and the student. Establishing a procedure for grading and taking the actual time to grade students' work is absolutely necessary in the school setting. When grading papers or special assignments, place the grades immediately in the grade book. You must keep a documented record of students' assignments. Establish your blueprint for success early.

TIP
If you use a day planner, calendar, pocket or desk calendar—mark important dates. Dates for turning in grades to the office is critical. There will be other important dates that you should mark on the calendar.

Record Keeping

Organizational management of records that adequately asses and document student progress are crucial. There are required records that vary from academic records and are apart of a teachers expected duties. Examples of records which may be kept are:

- **Grades**—use a master grade book and or progress charts. If using progress charts keep them in a notebook—easy to find and if you have more that one class, records are easy to track. The computer can be used to record grades. Some teachers use the computer and a back up grade book. Many school districts require you to use the computer for storing grades. Ask questions ahead of time concerning grading expectations. Regardless of the method used, remember the rules of confidentiality and at no time should the information be in sight of other students

- **Attendance**—kept inside the grade book or on a progress chart. Be sure to take daily attendance and keep those records accurate. As you give tests, record dates in which you give the test. Remember to erase students absences or tardies. Keep your attendance and test taking data accurate.

• **Records**—short term request—there will be times when you need to document who turned in permission or field trip notes. Permission slips are documents that require parents signatures and make sure you keep accurate records and are prepared for questions.

End of the year records-at the end of the school year you will have to do year in cumulative records. To do this, you will use information that you accumulate all year. Accuracy is important.

• **Homework**—during the beginning days of getting your room organized, ask your buddy teacher or the person who is the head of your department, the districts policy on homework and the school and department policy on homework. Remember that homework should be an extension of the classroom and previous skills should have been taught. Homework should not be a punishment tool or given as busy work. Whenever you give homework, it should be checked immediately. Do not give homework and then wait several days before returning to student. On the elementary level homework will come in many forms. It can be simple activities, and sometimes work given to get students in the routine of returning work. Also, the checking of homework could be stickers or check marks. Consider, as you progress from one grade levels — letter grades become very important to students. Keep a record of homework activities with dates. Homework is given to reinforce instructions and students' growth and mastery.

Documentation (Anecdotal Record Keeping)

This can be a tedious task but it can serve as insight to parents regarding their child's school progress or concerns; a helpful aid during parent conferences; strong measuring stick to pinpoint dramatic changes in student's behavior.

Good records about students should be objective; only write notes on things that actually occur. Be precise and to the point. Before you begin writing things about students, decide the format you want to use and where you want to store the information. Consider the following items:

- Computer usage—some information can be stored on computer disc. There are programs for student profiles and annotations that can be stored on your computer. If you put information on the computer—please secure it with a password.
- Spiral notebook—can be labeled with tabs. Tabs can be used for students names, class periods, or specific concerns.
- Index cards—use an index box to store your cards. The box can contain the alphabetical letters and you can put the student's names behind the tabs.
- Small memo pads are useful for writing quick notes. You will need to transfer notes over to your master sheets.

The usage of materials is immeasurable. Whatever format used, the information should be stored out of the reach of students. Students by nature are inquisitive, keep the information in a secure place. Always take time out to gather your thoughts at the end of the day. Antecdotal record keeping can provide insight and information for many concerns that other teachers may inquire about students.

Break Times, Recess and Hall Passing

Depending upon the grade level, break time can be very disruptive. In the lower grades, the teacher has a designated time within the framework of the school day to take rest room or water breaks. Of course, there is a designated time, yet all students are not programmed to use the restroom at the same time. There will always be exceptions to your rules—you are dealing with humans. Be flexible. Through experience you will be able to recognize real emergencies and will be able to act properly.

In the upper grades, classroom breaks are usually taken before classes start and right after lunch time. Schedules are adaptable to grade levels, schools, and existing policies and procedures. Some schools enforce hall passes. In the middle schools, hall passes and requests to be in the hallway is a crucial factor. You cannot allow students to be unsupervised when they should be in your classroom. Factors to keep in mind:

- Lower grade students are lined up to pass in the hallway. Younger students are told to follow the person in front of them. Always line your students up and pass on the right side of the hallway.

Restroom breaks can be challenging. Do not allow all the students to enter the restrooms at one time. Too many students in the restrooms will result in toilets overflowing, paper wads being thrown, water fights and of course, some students coming out with urine on their clothes.

Lower grade students enter the restroom one or two at a time. When coming out they get a drink and get back in line. They are asked to stand quietly and wait for the other class members to finish their restroom time.

Passes are valuable for students use if they need to go to the restrooms unsupervised. Some schools are quite adamant about students being out in the halls without an appropriate pass.

- Middle and High School students generally take their restroom breaks as they change classes-or move from one area to another. Usually there is a ten minute break time used for passing in the hallway. Restroom procedures are relative to grade levels, sites, and existing policies and procedures.

TIP

Check the school's policy on admitting students into the classroom if they are tardy. The first day of school, after the winter and spring breaks, or long holidays, establish or re-enforce your classroom routines, procedures, and expectations.

Do not be so overly anxious to teach that you sacrifice the need to establish classroom discipline. You cannot teach in a classroom where there is utter chaos. It is hard to gain control of your class once you let it get out of hand.

T IP

The first day of school and everyday thereafter, stand by your classroom door. Learn the names of the student's immediately. If you know there are students that are challenging —learn their names first.

Students are extremely smart and they can sense if you are uncomfortable or afraid of them. Students by nature, will enjoy trying to get teachers rattled or attempt to side track them in the classroom.

T IP

Student Code of Conduct-there should be an expected code of conduct for student behavior. Find out the district's policies and consequences. You should become immediately familiar with appropriate student behavior and consequences that should occur.

Substitute Teacher Planning

Leaving adequate plans for a substitute teacher can add continuity to your classroom and assist in keeping the students focused on a specific task or skill. Substitute lesson plans should be consistent to what the students are doing in the classroom. A student roster is crucial because students enjoy changing their names for a substitute teacher.

A classroom seating arrangement can ease a lot of frustration's for both the substitute teacher and the students. A time schedule detailing moving procedures, class changes, periods of movement, break times, lunch times, planning periods, and ending times are important information for a smooth day.

Often teachers request that the substitute follow the regular lesson plans; but invariably the students finish early. That is why you should plan supplemental or additional activities for the students. Some teachers will leave attached plans, book assignments, topics and page numbers as enrichment work. In some settings, teachers leave a variety of file folders with written instructions for use.

Leave a note for the substitute teacher with the names of teachers' in the area and next door that would be willing to give assistance. Leave a page in your planning that says—Notes from the Substitute Teacher—ask the substitute to leave you notes regarding the classes behavior, how much work the class accomplished, or information that would be of interest in your absence.

Lesson plans will need to be revised regularly. Students will move in and out of some of the classes and the academic focus will change. You cannot make a substitute folder and expect it to be applicable for the whole year.

ᑭARENTAL ᖾNVOLVEMENT

Working With Parents

Do not be afraid to let parents visit your classroom. Encourage parents to become part of your classroom. Teachers should not see parents as the enemy and should not be threatened by their presence; rather they should see the parents concern as sincere. Getting parents involved in education is the current emphasis. At one time, schools did not seek the parental involvement, now parents are needed to help make differences in the child's attitude and accomplishments in schools. Parents can be your best communicators to other parents. Many times the interaction of parents can be the catalyst that helps to get other parents involved.

The following tips will aid you immensely in planning activities and seeking parental involvement in your room:

- At the beginning of the schools year, set your goals and recruit parents as classroom assistance.
- Call parents and ask them if they would like to volunteer in your classroom. Have lists to refer to and tell them the kinds of activities that you have planned. When you see the parents on the first day of school, tell

them you will be in touch with them to volunteer. Follow up on your request for parent assistance.

• Plan your class activities for parents. Things should be well organized. Don't ask parents to assist in the classroom and you are not prepared.

• Caution—when asking parents to check papers, use symbols instead of names. Parents will naturally look for their child's work and will compare. Sometimes in their eagerness to help you, parents will tell other parents about their child's grades—thus causing unhealthy competition.

• Parents can sense if you are uncomfortable with them. Relax and make the parents feel welcomed.

Newsletters

On your master calendar, identify dates you would like to send a newsletter to parents. Correlate those dates with activities that are going on in school. Always be prepared to share grade card information and end of the semester dates and other school activities and information with the parent.

Decide what type of newsletter you would like to send to parents. There are a variety of programs available on the computer and on the internet that can assist you in developing fantastic newsletters. Other suggestions are:

• Beginning of the year introductory newsletter. Tell the parents something about yourself; share the goals for your classroom for the year. Make the newsletter short, precise and in a language that parents will understand. Highlight a few events for the month of August and September. Use this newsletter to ask for parent volunteers. Provide the school's telephone number, your planning period time and e-mail address. Let parent's know that you have an open door policy and they are always invited to visit in the classroom. When stating the goals for the students for the school year—keep it short and precise.

• During the course of the year, include: special testing times, anticipated field trips, parental involvement trips, upcoming school activities, special classroom activities, grade card days, conference times, textbooks information, student achievements, and in school assemblies.

Remember to keep the newsletter in an easy reading format, do not use too much educational jargon, keep it positive, and be consistent in sending a newsletter to parents. Do not schedule too many dates to send a newsletter and then forget to send one. Make scheduled dates to send information to parents.

TIP
In many schools, copies of all parent correspondence are sent to the office for approval before sending. Check your school's policy on sending out newsletters.

TEACHER PROFESSIONALISM

Benefits of Teacher Organizations

Participating in your professional organizations can help you to stay abreast of new ideas, trends, teaching methods, books and materials new or re-designed for the teaching field. Attending meetings not only helps with skill updates but it promotes teacher camaraderie with fellow educators and gives you a support base when you think there is a concern. Sometimes you may think you are the only one that is experiencing a problem in a certain area and in reality, the problem is not that acute.

Attending state conventions and professional meetings can help to re-vitalize you. Meetings will allow you to network with people not only in your school district but other school districts. You hear a different language and are provided exposure to view new materials for instruction. Many times meeting other educators, can strengthen your teaching skills and provide you with information to better meet the demands of teaching.

Whatever field you are in, there will be professional organizations that you can join. Don't let not having the money prevent you from becoming a member of viable organizations. In some organizations that you join, you will receive magazines, journals and monthly newsletter, information on conventions or special meetings. Additional places to look for classroom ideas and enhancements are: Teacher Resource Centers—which are available in some school districts, schools, school resource rooms, local teacher organizations, school district's professional development offices, fellow teachers in your building, school counselors, mentor teachers, principal's and district academic coordinators. The list is limitless—just ask questions.

Goals and Professional Development

When you embark upon your teaching career, the first thing you should do is set short and long range goals. Setting goals will help you to stay focused on your educational mission.

Long range goals are to help focus down the road. It is the road map that you follow until the end of the school year.

Your goal setting can help in your continued growth.

Meetings—participating in grade level committee meetings and state or local organizations can serve as information sources in staying abreast of what is going on in your academic arena. It also provides a time for you to network with other educators that will share the same feelings, attitudes, and concerns about students. It will be a brace in which you will not feel that you are alone. Often you will be rejuvenated when you share with people who have common goals. Participating in forums and study groups will be an opportunity for you to share and seek solutions to critical key issues. Many times the meetings will be held after school and it will be so easy to say, "I am so busy, I can't attend." Take time to grow in your profession.

Attend National conferences. Attendance will keep you on the cutting edge of new knowledge, new theories, techniques, and a time to preview the most current materials available in the subject you teach. It is so easy to say "I can't afford to attend." Sometimes you cannot put a price on your professional growth.

Read educational journals and books. The quest for knowledge will be everlasting. Utilize books, periodicals, and technology to provide a knowledge base to assist in keeping up with future trends.

Stress and Teaching

Learn to accept assistance from other teachers. Do not isolate yourself when you do not think things are going well. Do not feel overwhelmed with your teaching assignments. You are juggling teaching assignment, classroom management, diverse student needs, individuality in the classroom, behavior problems, personal issues, family situations, principal expectations, parent concerns, lack of enough time to actually teach the students, first year mentoring participation, department meeting schedules, after school commitments, and welcome to the real world-things are constantly evolving.

Stress is your reaction to everyday situations. It is how your body reacts. It is the wear and tear on your body system. In stressful situations, you may be short tempered, frustrated, tearful, or just depressed.

Physiological factors for stress can be: dry mouth, nervous stomach, rapid heartbeat, diarrhea or constipation, and muscular aches. Other behavior factors would be excessive eating, snacking, smoking, careless or reckless behavior/actions, loner in all activities, frowning, grinding of teeth, pacing or just extremely aggressive.

All stress is not bad. Some stressful situations can produce great ideas and perhaps positive changes. Remember to:
- Set aside time for yourself
- Eat well balanced meals and exercise
- Develop hobbies and spend time doing them
- Pleasure reading for relation or leisure
- Develop a social life or strengthen your family life

CHECKLIST
For Successful Activities, Task and Procedures

CHECKLIST
For Successful Activities, Task and Procedures

A well organized classroom is based on the teacher's ability to teach students procedures and essential materials for academic success. The number one problem in the classroom is not always discipline, but is the lack of procedures, routines and appropriate classroom consequences. As you review this checklist, use it to immediately grasp a situation and task and handle it with a minimum of stress.

First day jitters—the time finally comes and you are standing at your classroom door, waiting for students to enter. If you have prepared well and you have plenty of activities planned for the first day, then you will be a success. If you planned the bare minimum in activities and you hope you will have enough activities, then you are in trouble. When you look at the activities, please plan some acquaintance activities and be prepared to share something about yourself. Don't tell your life history; but share enough so the students will know you are human. Depending on the grade level, you may have prepared name tags. If you are teaching with older students, be prepared to let them find a place to sit in the classroom or ask them to sit in alphabetical order. If you are unsure, ask the students to pronounce their names. Nothing offends students more than mispronunciation of their names

If there are special supplies, have essential items in place. Have everything organized in your classroom. Place loose assignments in folders, label the folder and put in sequence, so every activity will flow. If you are putting class work on the board, put it on the board ahead of time. Start the very first day with a routine. Have your classroom routine visible. Go over classroom procedures and your expectation for students entering the classroom and preparing for work. Again, first year teachers are so eager to teach that they forget to repeat and go through the expectations, routines, and procedures of the class. Daily repetition of task, will save you headache in the long run. Take time at the very beginning of the school year to review procedures. It is very difficult to try and regain control once you lose control. This will make your first teaching job a frustrating experience, if you do not plan. Re-do what has not been done correctly for success.

At the end of every school day, take a few minutes at the end of day, and see the areas in which you were very successful. And then make improvements in the areas, in which you are concerned. If there is a dreaded task or class, see what the problem is and look for a solution. The problem will not go away. You will need to deal with it and you cannot wait and wait. You will need to tackle the situation. You cannot postpone finding a solution.

47

FIRST DAY OF SCHOOL JITTERS

	Dress for success
	Wear comfortable shoes
	Stand by door and greet students as they enter the classroom
	Say "Good morning" and "Good afternoon"
	Greet each student as they come in the door, ask how they enjoyed the summer break ,winter break, or vacation
	Act confident—do not exhibit nervousness

YOUR PREPARATION

	Your appearance and preparation
	Professionalism
	Project an attitude of confidence
	Knowledgeable of lesson
	Make a daily to do list
	Be excited about teaching
	Don't insult students with unconsciously negative body language. Make a mistake, admit it, apologize and move on
	Read the school policies

ROOM/SCHOOL AREAS

	Decorate your classroom
	Do you share materials
	Teacher's desk—what do you put inside and outside of your desk

	ROOM/SHOOL AREAS (con't)
	Student desk—cleanliness and what is kept in the desk
	Water fountain, bathroom, pencil sharpener procedures
	Learning spaces, centers, stations, group procedures
	Playground times and time to return to class
	Lunchroom duty and times
	Method in which you can get supplies ordered
	Flow and continuity of themes in your classroom or outside hall decorations
	BEGINNING CLASS
	Roll call, absentee procedures—scan class—learn how to streamline
	Tardy students, have a routine in place
	Classroom procedures in place—have a schedule
	Method in which materials will be distributed
	Each class has procedures to follow upon entering the room
	Review the time slot for classroom activities
	Review the student's names—if you cannot pronounce, ask for assistance
	FIRST 10 MINUTES OF CLASS ACTIVITIES
	Ask students to—
	Make a quick outline of their notes
	List important facts
	Quiz each other

✔ Checklist

	FIRST 10 MINUTES OF CLASS ACTIVITIES (Cont')
	Write a paragraph
	Predict the day's learning
	Draw a diagram, flow chart, or bar graph
	Make a set of flash cards
	Write a fact on the board
	WORK REQUIREMENTS
	Make necessary forms
	Heading papers—format to use
	Writing on back of paper
	Neatness, legibility
	Incomplete work bullets
	Placement of assignments—method to turn in homework
	Daily work list
	BASIC INSTRUCTIONAL APPROACHES
	Be familiar with whole group, individualized, and small group instruction
	Be familiar with various self paced learning and self instructional packages, tutorial audio tapes and worksheets, computer based instruction, and individualized inquiry investigations
	When utilizing cooperative learning, the three key features are: students work in groups, groups are heterogeneously formed, and reward systems are group oriented
	Engaged class time—amount of time the students actually work on the assignment
	Time on task—how much time is actually spent on engaged learning activities

CLASSROOM MANAGEMENT

	On task when entering room
	Daily routines
	Student movement procedures in place
	Always be prepared with materials—visuals, manipulative, etc
	Practiced classroom transition procedures—small group to large
	Effective ways to keep your classroom running smoothly
	Designated place for students' personal belongings
	Students should be responsible for keeping the classroom clean and orderly
	Time management strategies for students
	Have a syllabus or planner for class
	Procedures for cell phone usage
	Expect your low achievers to complete class work
	Labeling of students should be avoided
	Encourage students to keep track of their classroom achievements
	Create an organizational structure that will make sense to the students
	Design instruction so students can grasp ideas or meanings
	Write times on the board so students can become accustomed to completing task in a certain time frame

PREPARING LESSON PLANS—DISTRICT GOALS—STATE OBJECTIVES

	"Failing to plan means planning to fail"
	Know the State objectives for your grade level
	Know the expected students' outcomes
	Include enough vocabulary building
	Define what specific instructional strategies or activities will be used
	Check on the resources, such as supplementary books, audiovisual materials, speakers, and field trips
	What method of evaluation will be used
	Relate lesson plans to student experiences when possible
	Better to over plan
	Look for ways to extend students' thinking and involvement in multiple learning modalities
	Be familiar with Bloom's Taxonomy
	Use data to prepare classroom goals, activities and lesson planning
	Be prepared for students who will turn assignments in late— have procedures in place

INSTRUCTIONAL ACTIVITIES—STRATEGIES

	Use pacing calendar
	Signals for students' attention
	Signals for teacher's attention
	Address students talking during independent study
	Identify activities to do when work is completed

INSTRUCTIONAL ACTIVITIES—STRATEGIES (Con't)

	Procedure for students movement in and out of small group
	Identify materials for group work
	Expected behavior in group
	Expected behavior of students not in group
	Collaboration procedures for group work
	Daily agenda to follow
	Evidence of standards and benchmarks
	Understand and use Bloom's Taxonomy to push students to higher levels of thinking
	Use collected data for classroom improvement
	Develop questioning techniques that encourage students to think
	Provide materials, supplies, manipulatives, and appropriate materials for classroom use
	Remember to provide positive reinforcement and praise for all students
	Help students to develop the skills of visualizing when reading-assist them in creating mental pictures for task

TECHNOLOGY AWARENESS

	Learn to use the computer-constantly upgrade skills
	Utilize the computer for everyday classroom activities
	Do charts, class rosters, and other frequently used items on the computer/disk for easy retrieval
	Learn how to produce newsletters and fliers
	Take computer classes for upgrade in skills
	Use a removable disc stick to keep your back up material from your computer

INTERVENTION STRATEGIES

	Use every opportunity to augment school life with extracurricular activities
	Modify assignments—shorten assignments to fit student abilities
	Change seating arrangements
	Identify students strengths and use to meet their instructional needs
	Vary your lesson presentations
	Provide hands on activities
	Vary activities to meet learning styles
	Develop contract systems to work with students
	Expect your low achievers to complete class work
	Labeling of students should be avoided

CHECKLIST OF INTERVENTIONS

	Modify assignment—shorten assignments to fit student abilities
	Single step instructions (modify). Some students are only capable of processing one task at a time
	Change seating arrangement
	Develop a contract system
	One-to-one teacher/student interaction time (bi-weekly)
	Find the student's strength and use that as a motivator
	Praise good behavior
	Make visual motivators

CHECKLIST OF INTERVENTIONS (Con't)

	Vary ways you present lesson instructions to meet various learning styles
	Vary activities to meet learning style differences
	Pair with appropriate peer model
	Develop a system of organization for students
	Develop a plan of coping strategies students can use daily to help them understand "how to tackle and complete" assignments on their own. Train them at the beginning of the year until it becomes a habit
	Provide hands—on experiences; work with chalkboard, flash cards, tape player, computer, typewriter, and other materials.
	Use daily individual learning folders

CHECKING ASSIGNMENTS IN CLASS —PROCEDURES

	Students exchanging papers—caution
	Marking and grading assignments
	Turning in assignments

COMMUNICATION ASSIGNMENTS

	Returning assignments
	Homework assignments
	Make-up/late/extra credit work
	Parental update, newsletters, memos

GRADING PROCEDURES

	Student expectations and class goals explained
	Recording grades

GRADING PROCEDURES (Con't)

	Grading criteria's visible in the room
	Contracting with students for grades
	Method in which you provide accelerated class work

ASSESSMENT

	Define the criteria to use for assessment
	Use a variety of test techniques and classroom strategies
	Don't let the students see your frustration or stress regarding standardized testing
	Provide timely evaluation feedback to students
	Become familiar with portfolio assessment
	Do not use test as a threat to students
	Use the levels of Bloom's Taxonomy when developing test

ACADEMIC FEEDBACK

	Rewards and incentives
	Posting student work
	Communicating with parents
	Students' record of grades-keep accurate and up to date
	Written comments on assignments

INTERRUPTIONS

	Rules
	Talk amongst students
	Turning in assigned work

	INTERRUPTIONS (Con't)
	Returning assignments
	Out-of-seat policies
	Emergency procedures
	DISCIPLINE
	Entrance procedures into the classroom are in place
	Make the lesson meaningful
	Start the year with definite, imposed controls, which can be relaxed
	Make sure your room standards are fair, consistent, and enforceable
	Insist on students responding one at a time
	Avoid predicting or threatening specific punishments
	Don't make an issue out of everything
	Don't punish the whole class for the misbehavior of one or a few students
	Don't argue with students
	Compliment the class when warranted
	Have a sense of humor
	Be friendly—but remember there is a difference between friendliness and familiarity
	Don't be afraid to apologize or to make corrections
	Be aware of student seating arrangements
	Communicate with students' parents

	DISCIPLINE (Con't)
	Monitor your instructional techniques, where you work and walk in the classroom
	Speak to students with respect
	Take care of your desk, classroom, grading materials, and learning materials
	Be sure you can see all the students and they can see and hear you
	Be sure instructional displays and presentations can be seen by students
	Use a variety of instructional techniques to reach all students in the classroom
	Treat students with respect
	Refrain from threats or sarcasm
	Be fair, firm, and consistent with student relationships
	ENDING CLASS
	Putting away supplies, equipment
	Cleaning up the classroom
	Dismissing class procedures
	Homework procedures
	Closure for learning

Checklist

OTHER PROCEDURES

	Lunch procedures
	Student helpers and/or monitors
	Substitute plans in an obvious place for substitute to locate
	Playground/Hall duty times and locations
	Special need students—procedures in place
	Teacher Assistant procedures
	Names of students who leave the room for special classes or events
	Emergency, fire and disaster drills, and intruder procedures—know the differences

END OF THE DAY CLOSUDRE

	Review the day's events
	Identify the activities that were successful
	Write down any activities that you found uncomfortable
	Take a bird's eye view of the classroom—do you need to change anything in the room

TEAM TEACHING

	Two or more teachers will collaborately work together on a specific unit or subject area of knowledge
	Teaming is an opportunity for teachers to combine their expertise on certain subjects
	Students benefit when students are competent in their teaching fields
	Not all teachers can work well in a teaming atmosphere
	In team teaching, discipline procedures should be well defined and in place for all to follow

✓ Checklist

	BUILD STRONG RELATIONSHIPS WITH PARENTS
	Send positive communications home
	Call parents to share positive news
	Act quickly to involve parents if there are problems
	Document parents contacts
	Do not make parents feel uncomfortable
	Do not send handwritten correspondence hurriedly—it may contain misspelled words
	Keep correspondence to parents for your records
	Do not write a note to a parent if you are angry or upset in any form-you may regret the note at a later date
	TEACHER EVALUATIONS AND PROFESSIONAL DEVELOPMENT
	Find out about the evaluation instrument the administrator will use to evaluate you early
	Review your evaluations and make a personal growth plan
	Know the dates for evaluation and be prepared for classroom visitations
	Participate in district professional development activities
	Attend grade level meetings
	Attend state education meetings for professional growth— essential to being professional
	Consider obtaining National Board certification versus additional educational degrees

PROFESSIONALISM

	Set professional goals—short and long range
	Join professional organizations
	Read for continuous growth
	Display your teaching degree in your classroom

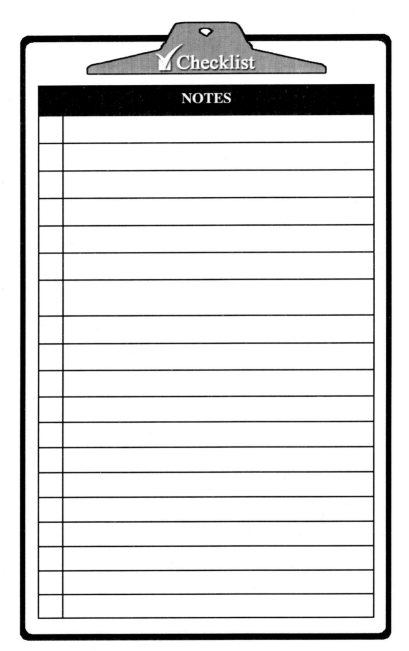

Checklist

NOTES

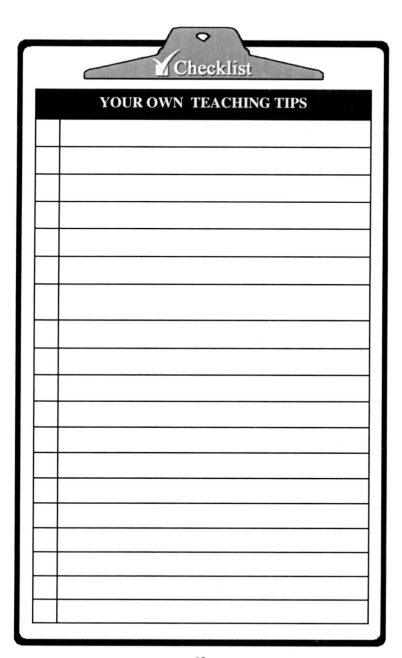

✔ Checklist

YOUR OWN TEACHING TIPS

TIPS FOR TEACHERS